SONGS FROM ALICE

Alice in Wonderland & Through the Looking-Glass

Words by LEWIS CARROLL

set to music by DON HARPER

with illustrations by CHARLES FOLKARD

HOLIDAY HOUSE · NEW YORK

Contents

The Little Crocodile

♩ = 82

Introduction

How doth the lit - tle croc - o - dile Im -

C7 / F / F / Gm7

prove his shin - ing tail, And pour the wat - ers of the Nile On

C7 / F (Fmaj7)(F7) / Bb / Dm7

ev - ery gol - den scale! How cheer-ful - ly he seems to grin, How

G7 / C7 / F / Gm7

rall.

neat-ly spread his claws, And wel-comes lit-tle fish - es in With gent-ly smil-ing jaws!

C7 / F (Fmaj7)(7) / Bb / C7 / Fm

Old Father William

♩ = 92

Flute, recorder ad lib.

Introduction

"You are old, Fath-er Will-iam," the

Dm7   G7   C7   F   F

young man said, "And your hair has be - come ve - ry white; And

B♭   B♭m   F   G9   Gm7   C7

yet you in - ces-sant-ly stand on your head, Do you think, at your age, it is right?

F   Fmaj7   F7   B♭6   B♭m6 (9)   Dm7   G7   C7   F

"In my youth," Father William replied to his son,
　"I feared it might injure the brain;
But, now that I'm perfectly sure I have none,
　Why, I do it again and again."

"You are old," said the youth, "as I mentioned before,
　And have grown most uncommonly fat;
Yet you turned a back-somersault in at the door—
　Pray, what is the reason of that?"

"In my youth," said the sage, as he shook his grey locks,
　"I kept all my limbs very supple
By the use of this ointment—one shilling the box—
　Allow me to sell you a couple."

continued overleaf

6

"You are old," said the youth, "and your jaws are too weak
   For anything tougher than suet;
Yet you finished the goose, with the bones and the beak—
   Pray, how did you manage to do it?"

"In my youth," said his father, "I took to the law,
   And argued each case with my wife;
And the muscular strength which it gave to my jaw,
   Has lasted the rest of my life."

"You are old," said the youth; "one would hardly suppose
   That your eye was as steady as ever;
Yet you balanced an eel on the end of your nose—
   What made you so awfully clever?"

"I have answered three questions, and that is enough,"
   Said his father; "Don't give yourself airs!
Do you think I can listen all day to such stuff?
   Be off, or I'll kick you downstairs!"

Twinkle, twinkle, little Bat

Pig and Pepper

Introduction and interlude

"Speak rough-ly to your lit-tle boy, And beat him when he snee-zes: He on-ly does it to an-noy Be-cause he knows it tea-ses."

CHORUS

Wow! Wow! wow! wow! wow! wow! wow! wow! wow! wow! wow! wow! wow! wow!

fine

"I speak severely to my boy,
  I beat him when he sneezes;
For he can thoroughly enjoy
  The pepper when he pleases!"

Chorus
  Wow! wow! wow!

10

The Lobster Quadrille

"You can really have no notion how delightful it will be,
When they take us up and throw us, with the lobsters, out to sea!"
But the snail replied, "Too far, too far!" and gave a look askance—
Said he thanked the whiting kindly, but he would not join the dance.
    Would not, could not, would not, could not, would not join the dance.
    Would not, could not, would not, could not, could not join the dance.

continued overleaf

"What matters it how far we go?" his scaly friend replied;
"There is another shore, you know, upon the other side.
The further off from England the nearer is to France—
Then turn not pale, beloved snail, but come and join the dance.
  Will you, won't you, will you, won't you, will you join the dance?
  Will you, won't you, will you, won't you, won't you join the dance?"

e dance?'

'Tis the Voice of the Lobster

tones of the Shark: But, when the tide ris - es and sharks are a - round, His

G7　　C　　Am7　　D7　　Dm7　　G7

1st time　　*2nd time*

voice has a tim-id and trem-u-lous sound.　　*fine*

Dm7　　Am7　　G7　　G7　　C　　C

I passed by his garden, and marked, with one eye,
How the Owl and the Panther were sharing a pie;
The Panther took pie-crust, and gravy, and meat,
While the Owl had the dish as its share of the treat.
When the pie was all finished, the Owl, as a boon,
Was kindly permitted to pocket the spoon:
While the Panther received knife and fork with a growl,
And concluded the banquet——

Beautiful Soup

The Queen of Hearts

Between Yourself and Me

♩. = 90

Flute, recorder ad lib.

Introduction

They told me you had been to her, And men-tioned me to him: She gave me a good cha-rac-ter, But said I could not swim. He tween your-self and me.

D   D   Dmaj7   D7   G   Em7   Bm7

1, 2, 3, 4 & 5   *last verse*   *fine*

E7   A7   Em7   A7   D

He sent them word I had not gone,
  (We know it to be true):
If she should push the matter on,
  What would become of you?

I gave her one, they gave him two,
  You gave us three or more;
They all returned from him to you,
  Though they were mine before.

If I or she should chance to be
  Involved in this affair,
He trusts to you to set them free,
  Exactly as we were.

My notion was that you had been
  (Before she had this fit)
An obstacle that came between
  Him, and ourselves, and it.

Don't let him know she liked them best,
  For this must ever be
A secret, kept from all the rest,
  Between yourself and me.

Jabberwocky

Introduction and interlude

'Twas brill-ig, and the sli - thy toves Did

gyre and gim - ble in the wabe; All mim-sy were the bor-o-goves, And

the mome raths out - grabe.

Last time only *(slower)* *fine*

"Beware the Jabberwock, my son!
  The jaws that bite, the claws that catch!
Beware the Jubjub bird, and shun
  The frumious Bandersnatch!"

He took his vorpal sword in hand:
  Long time the manxome foe he sought—
So rested he by the Tumtum tree,
  And stood awhile in thought.

And as in uffish thought he stood,
  The Jabberwock, with eyes of flame,
Came whiffling through the tulgey wood,
  And burbled as it came!

One, two! One, two! And through and through
  The vorpal blade went snicker-snack!
He left it dead, and with its head
  He went galumphing back.

"And hast thou slain the Jabberwock?
  Come to my arms, my beamish boy!
O frabjous day! Callooh! Callay!"
  He chortled in his joy.

'Twas brillig, and the slithy toves
  Did gyre and gimble in the wabe;
All mimsy were the borogoves,
  And the mome raths outgrabe.

Tweedledum and Tweedledee

♩ = 82

Introduction

Flute, recorder ad lib.

Twee-dle-dum and Twee-dle-dee A-

C   **Cmaj7**

greed to have a bat-tle; For Twee-dle-dum said Twee-dle-dee Had

C7   **F**   **Fm**

spoiled his nice new rat-tle. Just then flew down a mon-strous crow, As

G13   **C**   **Cmaj7**

black as a tar bar-rel; Which fright-ened both the her-oes so, They

C7   **F**   **Fm**

quite for-got their quar-rel.   *fine*

G7   **C**

The Walrus and the Carpenter

The moon was shining sulkily,
  Because she thought the sun
Had got no business to be there
  After the day was done—
''It's very rude of him,'' she said,
  ''To come and spoil the fun!''

The sea was wet as wet could be,
  The sands were dry as dry.
You could not see a cloud, because
  No cloud was in the sky:
No birds were flying overhead—
  There were no birds to fly.

continued overleaf

The Walrus and the Carpenter ~ *continued*

The Walrus and the Carpenter
  Were walking close at hand;
They wept like anything to see
  Such quantities of sand:
"If this were only cleared away,"
  They said, "it would be grand!"

"If seven maids with seven mops
  Swept it for half a year,
Do you suppose," the Walrus said,
  "That they could get it clear?"
"I doubt it," said the Carpenter,
  And shed a bitter tear.

continued overleaf

'T

"O Oysters, come and walk with us!"
  The Walrus did beseech.
"A pleasant walk, a pleasant talk,
  Along the briny beach:
We cannot do with more than four,
  To give a hand to each."

The eldest Oyster looked at him,
  But never a word he said:
The eldest Oyster winked his eye,
  And shook his heavy head—
Meaning to say he did not choose
  To leave the oyster-bed.

But four young Oysters hurried up,
    All eager for the treat:
Their coats were brushed, their faces washed,
    Their shoes were clean and neat—
And this was odd, because, you know,
    They hadn't any feet.

Four other Oysters followed them,
    And yet another four;
And thick and fast they came at last,
    And more, and more, and more—
All hopping through the frothy waves,
    And scrambling to the shore.

The Walrus and the Carpenter
    Walked on a mile or so,
And then they rested on a rock
    Conveniently low:
And all the little Oysters stood
    And waited in a row.

"The time has come," the Walrus said,
    "To talk of many things:
Of shoes—and ships—and sealing-wax—
    Of cabbages—and kings—
And why the sea is boiling hot—
    And whether pigs have wings."

"But wait a bit," the Oysters cried,
    "Before we have our chat;
For some of us are out of breath,
    And all of us are fat!"
"No hurry!" said the Carpenter:
    They thanked him much for that.

continued overleaf

Flute, recorder ad lib.

(after last verse only)

"A loaf of bread," the Walrus said,
   "Is what we chiefly need:
Pepper and vinegar besides
   Are very good indeed—
Now, if you're ready, Oysters dear,
   We can begin to feed."

"But not on us!" the Oysters cried,
   Turning a little blue.
"After such kindness, that would be
   A dismal thing to do!"
"The night is fine," the Walrus said.
   "Do you admire the view?"

"It was so kind of you to come!
  And you are very nice!"
The Carpenter said nothing but
  "Cut us another slice:
I wish you were not quite so deaf—
  I've had to ask you twice!"

"It seems a shame," the Walrus said,
  "To play them such a trick,
After we've brought them out so far,
  And made them trot so quick!"
The Carpenter said nothing, but
  "The butter's spread too thick!"

"I weep for you," the Walrus said:
  "I deeply sympathize."
With sobs and tears he sorted out
  Those of the largest size,
Holding his pocket-handkerchief
  Before his streaming eyes.

"O Oysters," said the Carpenter,
  "You've had a pleasant run!
Shall we be trotting home again?"
  But answer came there none—
And this was scarcely odd, because
  They'd eaten every one.

Humpty Dumpty

Little Fishes

In winter, when the fields are white, I
sing this song for your de-light. In
spring, when woods are get-ting green, I'll
try and tell you what I mean. In

In summer, when the days are long,
Perhaps you'll understand my song:

In autumn, when the leaves are brown,
Take pen and ink, and write it down.

I sent a message to the fish:
I told them "This is what I wish."

The little fishes of the sea,
They sent an answer back to me.

continued overleaf

The little fishes' answer was
"We cannot do it, Sir, because——"

I sent to them again to say
"It will be better to obey."

The fishes answered, with a grin,
"Why, what a temper you are in!"

I told them once, I told them twice:
They would not listen to advice.

I took a kettle large and new,
Fit for the deed I had to do.

My heart went hop, my heart went thump;
I filled the kettle at the pump.

Then someone came to me, and said
"The little fishes are in bed."

I said to him, I said it plain,
"Then you must wake them up again."

I said it very loud and clear;
I went and shouted in his ear.

But he was very stiff and proud;
He said "You needn't shout so loud!"

And he was very proud and stiff;
He said "I'd go and wake them, if——"

I took a corkscrew from the shelf:
I went to wake them up myself.

And when I found the door was locked,
I pulled and pushed, and kicked and knocked.

And when I found the door was shut,
I tried to turn the handle, but——

The Lion and the Unicorn

♩ = 98

Flute, recorder ad lib.

Introduction

The Li - on and the U - ni-corn were fight-ing for the crown; The Li - on beat the U - ni-corn all round the town. Some gave them white bread and some gave them brown; Some gave them plum cake and drummed them out of town.

Gm7　C7　F　A+7　Dm7

G　G7　Cmaj7　C　Am

Dm7　G7　Am　Am7　Dm9

fine

G7 (13)　C

A-Sitting on a Gate

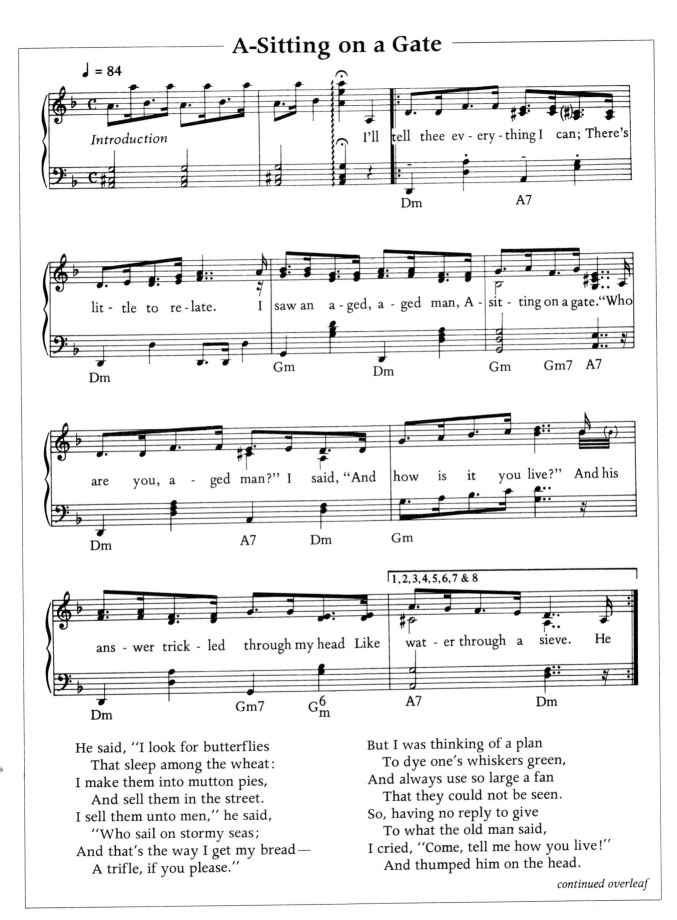

He said, "I look for butterflies
  That sleep among the wheat:
I make them into mutton pies,
  And sell them in the street.
I sell them unto men," he said,
  "Who sail on stormy seas;
And that's the way I get my bread—
  A trifle, if you please."

But I was thinking of a plan
  To dye one's whiskers green,
And always use so large a fan
  That they could not be seen.
So, having no reply to give
  To what the old man said,
I cried, "Come, tell me how you live!"
  And thumped him on the head.

continued overleaf

(before first verse only)

Dm   A7   Dm

Gm   Dm   Gm   Gm7   A7   Dm   A7   Dm

1, 2, 3, 4, 5, 6, 7 & 8

Gm   Dm   Gm7   G$_m^6$ A7   Dm

His accents mild took up the tale:
   He said, "I go my ways,
And when I find a mountain-rill,
   I set it in a blaze;
And thence they make a stuff they call
   Rowlands' Macassar Oil—
Yet twopence-halfpenny is all
   They give me for my toil!"

But I was thinking of a way
   To feed oneself on batter,
And so go on from day to day
   Getting a little fatter.
I shook him well from side to side,
   Until his face was blue:
"Come, tell me how you live," I cried,
   "And what it is you do!"

He said, "I hunt for haddocks' eyes
   Among the heather bright,
And work them into waistcoat-buttons
   In the silent night.
And these I do not sell for gold
   Or coin of silvery shine,
But for a copper halfpenny,
   And that will purchase nine.

continued overleaf

(before first verse only)

Dm A7 Dm

Gm Dm Gm Gm7 A7 Dm A7 Dm

1, 2, 3, 4, 5, 6, 7 & 8

Gm Dm Gm7 G⁶ₘ A7 Dm

"I sometimes dig for buttered rolls,
  Or set limed twigs for crabs;
I sometimes search the grassy knolls
  For wheels of Hansom-cabs.
And that's the way" (he gave a wink)
  "By which I get my wealth—
And very gladly will I drink
  Your Honour's noble health."

I heard him then, for I had just
  Completed my design
To keep the Menai bridge from rust
  By boiling it in wine.
I thanked him much for telling me
  The way he got his wealth,
But chiefly for his wish that he
  Might drink my noble health.

And now, if e'er by chance I put
  My fingers into glue,
Or madly squeeze a right-hand foot
  Into a left-hand shoe,
Or if I drop upon my toe
  A very heavy weight,
I weep, for it reminds me so Of

Queen Alice

Flute, recorder ad lib.

Introduction

To the Look-ing-Glass world it was Al-ice that said, "I've a scep-tre in hand, I've a crown on my head; Let the Look-ing-Glass crea-tures, what-ev-er they be, Come and dine with the Red Queen, the White Queen, and me!" (Then)

Then fill up the glasses as quick as you can,
And sprinkle the table with buttons and bran:
Put cats in the coffee, and mice in the tea—
And welcome Queen Alice with thirty-times-three!

continued overleaf

"O Looking-Glass creatures," quoth Alice, "draw near!
'Tis an honour to see me, a favour to hear:
'Tis a privilege high to have dinner and tea
Along with the Red Queen, the White Queen, and me!"

Then fill up the glasses with treacle and ink,
Or anything else that is pleasant to drink;
Mix sand with the cider, and wool with the wine—
And welcome Queen Alice with ninety-times-nine!

Hush-a-by Lady in Alice's Lap

♩ = 122

Flute, recorder ad lib.

Introduction

Hush - a - by Lad - y, in Al - i - ce's

G7   C   C   Am7   Dm7   G7

lap! Till the feast's read - y, we've time for a nap:

C   Cmaj7   Fmaj7   Dm7   C

When the feast's ov - er, we'll go to the ball — Red Queen, and

Em   Fmaj7   D7   G7   C   Fmaj7

fine

rall.

White Queen, and Al - ice, and all!

Em7   Am7   Dm7   G7   C

The Fish Riddle

♩. = 82

Flute, recorder ad lib.

(Introduction, interlude and coda)

Bell

F7   Bb   fine   Bb   Gm

"First the fish   must be caught."

C7   F7   Bb   Gm7

That is eas-y: a   ba-by, I think, could have caught it.   "Next, the fish

Bbm6   C9   F13   Bb

must be bought." That is eas-y: a pen-ny, I think, would have bought it.

"Now cook me the fish!"
That is easy, and will not take more than a minute.
"Let it lie in a dish!"
That is easy, because it already is in it!

"Bring it here. Let me sup!"
It is easy to set such a dish on the table.
"Take the dish-cover up!"
Ah, *that* is so hard that I fear I'm unable!

For it holds it like glue—
Holds the lid to the dish, while it lies in the middle:
Which is easiest to do,
Un-dish-cover the fish, or dishcover the riddle?

Index of first lines

© 1978 A. & C. Black Ltd.

Printed in the United States of America

First American publication 1979

Library of Congress Cataloging in Publication Data

Harper, Don.
  Songs from Alice.

  Children's songs; with chord symbols.
  Includes index.
  1. Children's songs. 2. Dodgson, Charles Lutwidge, 1832–1898—Musical settings. I. Folkard, Charles James, 1878-   II. Title
M1998.H [M1619.5.D49] 786.6'24'06
ISBN 0-8234-0358-0 79-11314